BIBLE
BASICS

*Summaries, Outlines,
and Key Verses of Every
Book in the Bible*

Dr. Daniel C. Russell

ISBN: 9781717243348

About Author

Dr. Daniel Russell, a graduate of Calvary Bible College, as well as Trinity Theological Seminary, and Bethany Divinity School, has more than 40 years of experience as a pastor, professor, and chaplain. His master's degree and doctorate are in Biblical Studies.

Dr. Russell has been an adjunct professor for Cornerstone University and Spring Arbor University in Michigan, as well as serving as a Police Chaplain, Hospice Chaplain, and Corporate Chaplain in Missouri, Kansas, and Michigan. He has been a certified Christian counselor for many years. He has also written numerous articles as a correspondent for GotQuestions.org. Many of the questions and answers are a feature of his web site. He also writes poetry that focuses on pastoral ministry, which is also on his web site. His web site can be accessed at www.pastordanrussell.com

Dr. Russell is also the author of "The Christ In Christian" and "Poetry by a Pastor".

Dedicated to

Ralph A. Nite, Sr.

*My first pastor, who first preached the basics of
the Bible to me*

Contents

BIBLE BOOK SUMMARIES

The Books of the Law

GENESIS is the book of beginnings as it records the creation of the heavens and earth, man, marriage, sin, sacrifice, nations, and government. We also see the fall of mankind, his deliverance, and God calling the Jews to be His people.

EXODUS is the story of how Israel became a nation as Moses led them out of bondage of Egyptian slavery. We also see the giving of the Ten Commandments and some of Israel's religious, as well as social, regulations.

LEVITICUS is an orderly account of how the Jews worshipped and how sinful people could approach a holy God through animal sacrifices. We also see the various offerings and feasts of Israel.

NUMBERS records Israel's forty years of wandering in the wilderness of Sinai because of their disobedience. We also see the numberings or censuses taken during this time.

DEUTERONOMY is the "second law" and is a review of the laws set forth by God through Moses in Exodus and Leviticus. This book also contains the Palestinian Covenant that reveals the geographical perimeters of Israel's land.

The Books of History

JOSHUA records the successor of Moses, Joshua, and his military campaigns as he led the Jews into the Promised Land of Canaan. We see the division of the land among the twelve tribes of Israel in this book.

JUDGES shows the backsliding of the Jews as a nation and their mixing with Canaanites religiously and socially. God raised up judges to lead the people, but they refused to follow.

RUTH is the romantic story of Ruth, a woman of Moab, who chooses to serve God with her mother-in-law, Naomi, in Israel. She meets and marries Boaz, who becomes her near kinsman in order to redeem her as his wife.

I SAMUEL shows the rise of Israel after they chose to have a king rule over them. The key characters in this book include Samuel, the prophet, and the kings, Saul and David.

II SAMUEL describes the forty-year reign of David over Israel with seven years in Hebron and thirty-three years in

Jerusalem. This book records David's sin with Bathsheba and the failure of his son Absalom.

I KINGS is the account of the reign of King Solomon and how the Kingdom was divided after his backsliding. The book traces the first dual kings, Jeroboam and Rehoboam, through the last dual kings, Ahab and Jehoshaphat.

II KINGS reveals the final decline and fall of Israel in 722 B.C. and then Judah in 586 B.C. The book covers four hundred years and gives us the setting for the Prophetical books.

I CHRONICLES reviews the reign of David and preparations for building the Temple. Many genealogies are recorded in this book, thus giving an accurate account of the lineage of Judaism.

II CHRONICLES continues the history of Israel up through Solomon's reign and Concentrates on the southern kingdom of Judah. This book closes with the decree of Cyrus when the Jews were allowed to return to the land from captivity.

EZRA shows the return of the Jews from Babylon after the decree of Cyrus in 536 B.C. with one group being led by Zerubbabel and another group (78 years later) being led by Ezra. The Temple is rebuilt during this time.

NEHEMIAH recounts the rebuilding of Jerusalem's walls under the leadership of Nehemiah, the governor, some fourteen years after Ezra. There is also the reinstating of sacrifices and feasts during this time.

ESTHER shows God's providential care for the Jews through Esther and Mordecai during a time in Persia when many Jews had voluntarily remained in Exile.

The Books of Poetry

JOB is the true story of a righteous man who lived before the time of Abraham and was permitted to go through the loss of his possessions, family, and his health in order to show his faithfulness to God.

PSALMS is a collection of Hebrew songs that promote communion with God through praise and prayer. Most are written by David, but some are written by others. Some of the psalms are Messianic, predicting the coming Messiah/ Jesus.

PROVERBS is a collection of pithy sayings that apply divine wisdom to the practical problems of life. Many of the Proverbs contrast righteousness and unrighteousness, as well as wisdom and folly.

ECCLESIASTES was written by Solomon when he was backsliding from God and shows his perspective of the futility of life from a human vantage point apart from God. This book does contain some positive truths, but, for the most part, is the perspective of a carnal believer.

SONG OF SOLOMON is the romantic story of Solomon and his bride-to-be, who is a Shulamite woman. This book represents God's love for Israel as well as all people.

The Books of Prophecy

ISAIAH warns of coming judgment on the southern tribes of Judah and then records this judgment later in the book when the Babylonians invade. The book also records the fall of the ten northern tribes to Assyrian captivity earlier. Much of Isaiah is Messianic.

JEREMIAH was written during the later decline and fall of Judah to the Babylonians and Jeremiah weeps over the Jews' rejection of Jehovah. The prophet finally encourages surrender to Nebuchadnezzar.

LAMENTATIONS is Jeremiah's lament over the destruction of Jerusalem by the Babylonians and portrays God's lament over this necessary act of divine chastisement.

EZEKIEL writes of Jerusalem's impending fall in 586 B.C. and, then, he predicts its future restoration (even year future for today). The book is prophetic and includes many visions.

DANIEL was a young man deported in the Babylonian exile and, while in Babylon, he interprets dreams to the king there. The book is historic as well as prophetic in nature and gives us insight into the future chastisement and restoration of Israel.

HOSEA begins the Minor Prophets and describes, through Hosea's poor marriage with Gomer, Israel's unfaithfulness, chastisement, and restoration.

JOEL is one of the earliest prophets (c825 B.C.) and speaks of the coming Day of the Lord. The recorded locust plague foreshadows the coming judgment of God on Israel before He restores them.

AMOS, a herdsman turned prophet, tells Israel and surrounding nations of God's inevitable judgment on sin. This book was written in a period of material prosperity, but moral decay.

OBADIAH pronounced God's judgment against Israel's neighboring country of Edom, the home of the descendants of Esau. The setting is Edom in the Day of the Lord.

JONAH is the true account of the prophet Jonah's commission to preach in Nineveh, his fleeing from God, his second opportunity, the revival in Nineveh, and Jonah's misunderstanding with God. This book shows God's love and mercy toward the Gentiles.

MICAH was a contemporary of Isaiah and prophesied against Israel. The Jews' sins are seen as deserving of judgment. Also, Micah foretells the birthplace of Christ some 700 years beforehand.

NAHUM foretells the certain destruction of Nineveh some 150 years after Jonah's day and proves the principle of God's delay of judgment when He is honored.

HABAKKUK reveals the concept that God will punish a sinful nation by an even more sinful nation as the Chaldeans invade Judah. This book's theme is "the just shall live by faith".

ZEPHANIAH predicts judgment on Judah, which is a picture of the day of the Lord to come in the future against Israel. After both judgments there is restoration predicted as well.

HAGGAI is the first Minor Prophet after the exile and urges the Jews to resume rebuilding of the Temple after a delay of fifteen years. Haggai also predicts the final overthrow of Gentile world power

ZECHARIAH is the prophet who reveals the advent of Christ beforehand as well as encouraging the Jews to complete the Temple and get back to God.

MALACHI exhorts the people of Israel against spiritual ignorance and foretells the coming of John the Baptist. This book is the last one before the 400 "silent years".

The Gospels and Acts

MATTHEW is the Gospel that promises Messiah's arrival and records His ultimate rejection. This book focuses on Christ as King of the Jews and quotes the Old Testament often.

MARK presents Christ as Servant and is the most rapid and concise of the four Gospels. This book begins with Christ's ministry, not His birth, and is directed toward the Roman reader.

LUKE sees Christ as the perfect Man and is the most detailed of the accounts. This book reflects a historical style and shows how the story of salvation is HIStory.

JOHN stresses Christ as the Son of God and is distinct from the other three Gospels. John sees Christ as God in the flesh and the Author of eternal life to all of mankind.

ACTS chronicles the growth in the early church from Christ's ascension to Paul's Roman imprisonment (about 33 years). These are the "acts of the Holy Spirit" as men such as Peter and Paul preach the Gospel to Jews and Gentiles.

The Pauline Epistles

ROMANS is a systematic presentation of the Gospel with emphasis on salvation by grace through faith alone. The book reveals the doctrinal and practical truth of God's plan for mankind.

I CORINTHIANS is a letter written to correct errors in Christian conduct in the local church, such as dissension, immorality, marriage and remarriage, lawsuits, and general church disorder.

II CORINTHIANS is Paul's defense of the true Gospel and his true apostleship. This book speaks of Paul's experiences in the ministry as well as the subject of stewardship.

GALATIANS is a message to counteract the error of mixing the Jewish law and the grace of Christ's salvation. The theme is "justification by faith" and parallels the message of Romans.

EPHESIANS is an epistle of Christian living and encourages the believer who is "in Christ" to "put on the new man" and "walk worthy" of his calling as a Christian. The concept of the universal church is discussed in this book as well.

PHILIPPIANS is an epistle of Paul where he calls upon the believer to rejoice in Christ and display "proper Christian heart-mind attitudes". This book records the Gospel's advent into Europe.

COLOSSIANS is set forth to combat the early church error of Gnosticism, which denied the full deity and humanity of Christ. This book stresses Christ as Head of the Church as well as Head of the whole universe.

I THESSALONIANS contains the counsel of Paul in regard to Christian living with an emphasis on the return of the Lord in the "rapture" of the church.

II THESSALONIANS further clarifies the Lord's return to earth the seven-year period that will begin with the coming of the man of sin, and the practical implications of these truths to the believer.

I TIMOTHY is the first of the Pastoral Epistles and stresses sound doctrine, orderly church government, and principles for church members to live by.

II TIMOTHY describes the true servant of Christ, using Paul and Timothy as examples, as well as warning that "apostasy" has already set in during these last days. The remedy against all error is seen as the Word of God.

TITUS is Paul's commendation and charge to Titus, the young minister on the island of Crete. The theme embodies the charge to uphold sound doctrine and live godly lives.

PHILEMON is the apostle Paul's intercession to Philemon, a slave owner, on behalf of Onesimus, Philemon's runaway slave who had become a Christian. This book's message illustrates forgiveness through Christ.

HEBREWS presents the pre-eminence of Christ over Judaism with its sacrifices, priests, and dead works. Christ is seen as the ultimate High Priest and only true Mediator between God and man.

The General Epistles

JAMES is the first of the general epistles and one of the earliest books written. James is teaching the Hebrew Christians about true faith that produces works, while not contradicting the doctrine of salvation by faith alone.

I PETER is a letter of comfort and encouragement to Christians who were suffering persecution from non-Christians. Peter exhorts believers to grow spiritually in spite of suffering.

II PETER is a warning against the dangers of false teaching within the church and is written shortly before Peter's death. The end of the age is discussed in this book as the "heavens and earth burn with fervent heat".

I JOHN is written to counteract Gnosticism, which denied the truth about Christ. The themes of love, forgiveness, brotherly unity, and assurance of salvation are discussed in the book. The word "know" is repeated often in the book as well.

II JOHN warns against any compromise with doctrinal error and emphasizes that Christians should guard the truth with loving firmness.

III JOHN seems to balance II John's message in that this third letter stresses fellowship and hospitality to those who are "real" believers.

JUDE is another warning against apostasy and false doctrine and is similar in theme to II Peter. False teachers are described in detail in this book.

The Book of Prophecy

REVELATION records the climactic events of world history and amplifies the prophecy of Daniel and other prophets of the Old Testament. This prophecy includes the seven churches, the judgments of the seals, trumpets, and bowls, and the ultimate return of Christ to the earth.

BIBLE BOOK
OUTLINES

Genesis

I. (1-3) REDEMPTION STAGED

    A. (1) THE CREATION STORY
    B. (2-3) THE CREATION AND FALL OF MAN

II. (4-11) REDEMPTION NEEDED

    A. (4-5) MURDER AND DEATH
    B. (6-9) DISOBEDIENCE AND JUDGMENT
    C. (10-11) REBELLION AND CONFUSION

III. (12-50) REDEMPTION VIA ISRAEL

    A. (12-23) ABRAHAM
    B. (24-27) ISAAC
    C. (28-36) JACOB
    D. (37-50) JOSEPH

EXODUS

I. (1-12) MOSES FACES PHARAOH

    A. (1-4) MOSES' LIFE AND CALL
    B. (5-12) THE PLAGUES ON EGYPT

II. (13-18) MOSES FACES THE PEOPLE

    A. (13-15:22) THE PARTING OF THE RED SEA
    B. (15:23-17:7) THE WATER AND THE MANNA
    C. (17:8-17:16) THE BATTLE WITH THE AMALEKITES
    D. (18) THE COUNSELING OF JETHRO

III. (19-40) MOSES FACES GOD

    A. (19-24) GOD GIVES THE LAW
    B. (25-31) GOD GIVES THE TABERNACLE
    C. (32-35) MAN BREAKS THE LAW
    D. (36-40) MAN BUILDS THE TABERNACLE

LEVITICUS

I. (1-10) THE CONSECRATION OF THE JEWS

    A. (1-5) THE FIVE OFFERINGS
    B. (6-7) THE LAWS GOVERNING OFFERINGS

C. (8-9)   THE LAWS GOVERNING PRIESTS
D. (10)   THE EXAMPLE OF NADAB & ABIHU

II. (11-27)   THE CONDUCT OF THE JEWS

A. (11)   IN REFERENCE TO DIET
B. (12)   IN REFERENCE TO CHILDBIRTH
C. (13-15)   IN REFERENCE TO LEPROSY
D. (16-17)   IN REFERENCE TO THE DAY OF ATONEMENT
E. (18-20)   IN REFERENCE TO OTHERS
F. (21-22)   IN REFERENCE TO PRIESTS
G. (23)   IN REFERENCE TO FEASTS
H. (24-27)   IN REFERENCE TO THE LAND

NUMBERS

I. (1-10:10)   THE JOURNEY BEGINS

A. (1)   THE NUMBERING IN THE WILDERNESS
B. (2)   THE ENCAMPMENT IN THE WILDERNESS
C. (3-4)   THE LEVITES IN THE WILDERNESS
D. (5-8)   THE PEOPLE IN THE WILDERNESS

DEUTERONOMY

I. (1-4) A SECOND LOOK AT THE JOURNEY

    A. (1)   FROM SINAI TO KADESH
    B. (2-3) FROM KADESH TO MOAB
    C. (4)   INTO THE LAND OF CANAAN

II. (5-26) A SECOND LOOK AT THE LAW

    A. (5-6)   THE COMMANDS TO TEACH THE LAW
    B. (7)   THE COMMANDS TO BE SEPARATED
    C. (8-12) THE COMMANDS TO HEED GOD'S WORD
    D. (13-26) THE COMMANDS FOR LIFE IN THE LAND

III. (27-30) A SECOND LOOK AT THE PROMISE

    A. (27)   THE PROMISE OF BLESSINGS AND CURSINGS
    B. (28)   THE PROMISE OF REWARDING OBEDIENCE
    C. (29-30) THE PROMISE OF THE LAND

IV. (31-34)   A SECOND LOOK AT MOSES

    A. (31)   MOSES' COUNSEL TO LEVITES AND TO JOSHUA
    B. (32)   MOSES' SONG TO GOD
    C. (33)   MOSES' BLESSINGS OF ISRAEL
    D. (34)   MOSES' DEATH

Joshua

I. (1-5)   THE PROMISED LAND IS ENTERED

    A. (1)   THE PATHWAY TO SUCCESS
    B. (2-4)   THE POWER FOR SUCCESS
    C. (5:1-12) THE PEOPLE FOR SUCCESS
    D. (5:13-15) THE POTENTATE FOR SUCCESS

II. (6-12)   THE PROMISED LAND IS CONQUERED

    A. (6-9)   THE CENTRAL CAMPAIGN
    B. (10)   THE SOUTHERN CAMPAIGN
    C. (11)   THE NORTHERN CAMPAIGN
    D. (12)   THE SUMMARY OF THE BATTLES

III. (13-21)   THE PROMISED LAND IS DIVIDED

    A. (13)   REUBEN, GAD, AND MANASSEH
    B. (14)   CALEB
    C. (15)   JUDAH
    D. (16-19) THE REST
    E. (20)   THE CITIES OF REFUGE
    F. (21)   THE LEVITES

IV. (22-24)   THE PROMISED LAND IS ENJOYED

   A. (22)   NO DIVISIONS
   B. (23)   NO TRANSGRESSIONS
   C. (24)   NO IDOLATRY

JUDGES

I. (1-2)   THE CAUSE OF THE CYCLE OF THE SIN

   A. (1)   ONLY PARTIAL VICTORY
   B. (2)   ONLY PARTIAL AFFECTION

II. (3-16)   THE JUDGES WITHIN THE CYCLE OF SIN

   A.   (3:1-11)   OTHNIEL
   B.   (3:12-31)   EHUD
   C.   (4-5)   DEBORAH/BARAK
   D.   (6-8:32)   GIDEON
   E.   (8:33-9:57) ABIMELECH
   F.   (10-12)   JEPHTHAH
   G.   (13-16)   SAMSON

III. (17-21)   THE RESULTS OF THE CYCLE OF SIN

   A. (17-18)   RELIGIOUSLY
   B. (19)   MORALLY
   C. (20-21)   POLITICALLY

RUTH

I. (1:1-18)   RUTH LEAVES MOAB

    A. (1:1-5)   NAOMI LEAVES MOAB
    B. (1:6-14)   ORPAH LEAVES MOAB
    C. (1:15-18) RUTH LEAVES MOAB

II. (1:19-2:23)   RUTH GOES TO BETHLEHEM

    A. (1:19-22) THE RETURN TO BETHLEHEM
    B. (2:1-7)   THE REQUEST TO GLEAN THE FIELD
    C. (2:8-13)   THE REWARD TO RUTH
    D. (2:14-16) THE REFRESHMENT FOR RUTH
    E. (2:17-23) THE REPORT TO NAOMI

III. (3:1-18)   RUTH'S DISCOVERY OF BOAZ AS HER NEAR KINSMAN

    A. (3:1-5)   THE DESIRE OF NAOMI
    B. (3:6-13)   THE DECISION OF BOAZ
    C. (3:14-18) THE DECLARATION OF RUTH

IV. (4:1-22)   RUTH'S REDEMPTION BY BOAZ AS HER NEAR KINSMAN

    A. (4:1-6)   THE REHEARSAL OF THE FACTS
    B. (4:7-12)   THE REDEMPTION OF RUTH

C. (4:13-17) THE RESTORER OF LIFE
D. (4:18-22) THE RESULTS OF THE MARRIAGE

FIRST SAMUEL

I. (1-8) SAMUEL AND ELI

   A. (1) THE BIRTH OF SAMUEL
   B. (2) THE JUDGMENT OF ELI
   C. (3) THE COMMISSION OF SAMUEL
   D. (4-7) THE DEATH OF ELI AND THE MINISTRY
       OF SAMUEL
   E. (8) THE PEOPLE'S REQUEST FOR A KING

II. (9-15) SAMUEL AND SAUL

   A. (9) SAUL IS CHOSEN
   B. (10) SAUL IS ANOINTED
   C. (11-12) THE MONARCHY IS ESTABLISHED
   D. (13-15) SAUL IS A SINFUL KING

III. (16-31) SAUL AND DAVID

   A. (16) DAVID IS CHOSEN AS KING
   B. (17) DAVID DEFEATS GOLIATH
   C. (18-26) SAUL CHASES DAVID
   D. (27-30) DAVID AMONG THE GENTILES
   E. (31) THE DEATH OF SAUL

SECOND SAMUEL

I. (1-10) DAVID AND HIS TRIUMPHS

    A. (1-4) KING DAVID IN HEBRON
    B. (5-10) KING DAVID IN JERUSALEM

II. (11-21) DAVID AND HIS TROUBLES

    A. (11-12) TROUBLES BETWEEN DAVID AND BATHSHEBA
    B. (13-14) TROUBLES BETWEEN AMNON AND ABSALOM
    C. (15-19) TROUBLES BETWEEN DAVID AND ABSALOM
    D. (20-21) TROUBLES BETWEEN DAVID AND HIS ENEMIES

III. (22-24) DAVID AND HIS TESTIMONY

    A. (22) DAVID'S SONG OF DELIVERANCE
    B. (23) DAVID'S MIGHTY MEN
    C. (24) DAVID'S LOVING HEART

FIRST KINGS

I. (1:1-2:12) DAVID DIES

A. (1:1-4)   DAVID'S ILLNESS
B. (1:5-53)   DAVID'S SUCCESSOR
C. (2:1-9)   DAVID'S CHARGE
D. (2:10-12) DAVID'S DEATH

II. (2:13-11:43) SOLOMON REIGNS

A. (2:13-46) SOLOMON'S INITIAL LEADERSHIP
B. (3)   SOLOMON'S CHOICE
C. (4)   SOLOMON'S WEALTH AND WISDOM
D. (5-8)   SOLOMON'S LABORS
E. (9-10)   SOLOMON'S KINGDOM
F. (11)   SOLOMON'S FOLLY

III. (12:1-16:28) THE KINGDOM DIVIDED

A. (12)   DIVISION INEVITABLE
B. (13-14:20)   ISRAEL'S KING, JEROBOAM
C. (14:21-31)   JUDAH'S KING, REHOBOAM
D. (15:1-8)   ABIJAM (JUDAH)
E. (15:9-24)   ASA (JUDAH)
F. (15:25-34)   NADAB (ISRAEL)
G. (16:1-14)   ELAH (ISRAEL)
H. (16:15-20)   ZIMRI (ISRAEL)
I. (16:21-28)   OMRI (ISRAEL)

IV. (16:29-22:53)   ELIJAH DECLARES

A. (16:29-34) THE SINS OF AHAB

SECOND KINGS

III. (9:11-17:41) THE DIVIDED KINGDOM'S LAST
                   DAYS

  A. (9:11-10:36)   JEHU (ISRAEL)
  B. (11)   ATHALIAH (JUDAH)
  C. (12)   JEHOASH (JUDAH)
  D. (13:1-9)   JEHOAHAZ (ISRAEL)
  E. (13:10-25)   JEHOASH (ISRAEL)
  F. (14:1-22)   AMAZIAH (JUDAH)
  G. (14:23-29)   JEROBOAM II (ISRAEL)
  H. (15:1-7)   AZARIAH (JUDAH)
  I. (15:8-12)   ZECHARIAH (ISRAEL)
  J. (15:13-15)   SHALLUM (ISRAEL)
  K. (15:16-22)   MENAHEM (ISRAEL)
  L. (15:23-26)   PEKAHIAH (ISRAEL)
  M. (15:27-31)   PEKAH (ISRAEL)
  N. (15:32-38)   JOTHAM (JUDAH)
  O. (16)   AHAZ (JUDAH)
  P. (17)   HOSHEA (ISRAEL)

IV. (18-25)   THE SINGLE KINGDOM'S LAST DAYS

  A. (18:1-20:21)   HEZEKIAH
  B. (21:1-26)   MANASSEH
  C. (22:1-23:30)   JOSIAH
  D. (23:31-33)   JEHOAHAZ
  E. (23:34-24:6)   JEHOIAKIM
  F. (24:7-16)   JEHOIACHIN
  G. (24:17-25:7)   ZEDEKIAH
  H. (25:8-30)   THE FINAL CAPTIVITY

FIRST CHRONICLES

I. (1-9)   GENEALOGIES

    A. (1)   ADAM TO THE SONS OF ESAU
    B. (2)   THE SONS OF ISRAEL
    C. (3-8)   THE SONS OF THE SONS OF ISRAEL
    D. (9)   OTHERS

II. (10)   SAUL

    A. (10:1-6)   SAUL'S SUICIDE
    B. (10:7-12)   SAUL'S SHAME
    C. (10:13-14)   SAUL'S SINS

III. (11-29)   DAVID

    A. (11:1-9)   DAVID AS KING

    B. (11:10-12:40) DAVID AND HIS MIGHTY MEN
    C. (13)   THE CURSE OF THE ARK OF THE COVENANT
    D. (14)   THE PHILISTINES ARE DE-FEATED
    E. (15-16)   THE BLESSINGS OF THE ARK OF THE COVENANT
    F. (17)   THE DESIRE OF DAVID
    G. (18-20)   VARIOUS KINGS DEFEATED
    H. (21)   DAVID'S SIN OF NUMBER-ING THE PEOPLE

I.   (22-27)   THE TEMPLE IS PREPARED
J.   (28-29)   DAVID'S LAST WORDS

SECOND CHRONICLES

I.   (1-9) THE KINGDOM UNITED UNDER SOLOMON

   A. (1)   SOLOMON'S PRAYER FOR WISDOM
   B. (2)   SOLOMON'S PREPARATION FOR THE
            TEMPLE
   C. (3-4)   SOLOMON'S PLAN FOR THE TEMPLE
   D. (5-7)   SOLOMON'S DEDICATION OF THE
            TEMPLE
   E. (8-9)   SOLOMON'S FAME

II. (10-12)   THE KINGDOM DIVIDED

   A. (10:1-11)   THE WRONG COUNSEL TAKEN
   B. (10:12-19) THE REBELLION OF JEROBOAM
   C. (11)   THE STRIFE OF THE DIVIDED
             KINGDOM
   D. (12)   THE SIN OF REHOBOAM

III. (13-35)   THE KINGDOM OF JUDAH

   A. (13)   ABIJAH
   B. (14-16)   ASA

C. (17-20)   JEHOSHAPHAT
D. (21)   JEHORAM
E. (22:1-9)   AHAZIAH
F. (22:10-23:21) ATHALIAH
G. (24)   JOASH
H. (25)   AMAZIAH
I. (26)   UZZIAH
J. (27)   JOTHAM
K. (28)   AHAZ
L. (29-32)   HEZEKIAH
M. (33:1-20)   MANASSEH
N. (33:21-25)   AMON
O. (34-35)   JOSIAH

IV. (36)   THE KINGDOM'S FINAL OVERTHROW

A. (36:1-4)   JEHOAHAZ BY EGYPT
B. (36:5-8)   JEHOIAKIM BY BABYLON
C. (36:9-10)   JEHOIACHIN BY BABYLON
D. (36:11-21)   ZEDEKIAH BY BABYLON
E. (36:22-23)   A RAY OF LIGHT IN THE
                DARKNESS

EZRA

I. (1-6)   ZERUBBABEL'S WORK ON THE TEMPLE

A. (1)   THE DECREE TO RETURN
B. (2)   THE PEOPLE WHO RETURNED
C. (3:1-7) THE WORSHIP OF THE PEOPLE
D. (3:8-13) THE WORK OF THE PEOPLE
E. (4)   THE OPPOSITION TO THE WORK
F. (5)   THE EXHORTATION TO WORK
G. (6)   THE COMPLETION OF THE WORK

II. (7-10) EZRA'S WORK WITH THE PEOPLE

A. (7)   THE MAN EZRA
B. (8:1-21) THE PEOPLE WHO FOLLOWED EZRA
C. (8:22-36) THE RETURN OF EZRA AND THE PEOPLE
D. (9-10) THE PEOPLE ARE SEPARATED FROM THE GENTILES

NEHEMIAH

I. (1-2) NEHEMIAH REMEMBERS

A. (1)   NEHEMIAH'S PRAYER TO GOD
B. (2:1-8) NEHEMIAH'S PLEA TO THE KING
C. (2:9-20) NEHEMIAH'S PLAN FOR THE WORK

II. (3-7) NEHEMIAH REBUILDS THE WALLS

A. (3)   THE RECORD OF THE WORKERS
B. (4-6) THE RESPONSE OF THE OPPOSITION
C. (7)   THE REGISTERING OF THE PEOPLE

III. (8-13) NEHEMIAH AND THE REVIVAL OF THE
 PEOPLE

    A. (8) REVIVAL AS THE LAW OF GOD IS
 READ

    B. (9) REVIVAL AS THE PEOPLE CON-
 FESS THEIR SINS

    C. (10-11) REVIVAL AS REFORMS ARE MADE

    D. (12) REVIVAL RESULTS IN THE
 DEDICATION OF THE WALLS

    E. (13) REVIVAL MAINTAINS AS OTHER
 REFORMS ARE MADE

ESTHER

I. (1-2) ESTHER BECOMES QUEEN

    A. (1) VASHTI IS OUT

    B. (2) ESTHER IS IN

II. (3) HAMAN BECOMES IRATE

    A. (3:1-6) THE REASON HAMAN IS IRATE

    B. (3:7-11) THE REQUEST HAMAN MAKES
 OF THE KING

    C. (3:12-15) THE RECORDING OF HAMAN'S
 IRATE REMARKS

III. (4-8)   THE JEWS ARE SAVED FROM
             ANNIHILATION

   A. (4)   THE JEWS FAST
   B. (5)   ESTHER SHOWS COURAGE
   C. (6)   MORDECAI IS REWARDED
   D. (7)   HAMAN IS PUNISHED
   E. (8)   THE JEWS ARE PRESERVED

IV. (9-10)   THE JEWISH CELEBRATION OF PURIM
             BEGINS

   A. (9:1-10)   THE JEWS ARE VICTORIOUS
   B. (9:11-16)   THE JEWS RESTED FROM
                 THEIR ENEMIES
   C. (9:17-32)   THE FEAST OF PURIM
                 INTRODUCED
   D. (10:1-3)   THE ADVANCEMENT OF
                MORDECAI

Job

III. (32-42)   JOB AND HIS ENCOUNTER WITH GOD

    A. (32-37)   THE MONOLOGUE OF ELIHU
    B. (38-42:6)   THE REVELATION OF GOD
    C. (42:7-17)   THE VINDICATION OF JOB

PSALMS

I.	(Psalms 1-41)	BOOK I
II.	(Psalms 42-72)	BOOK II
III.	(Psalms 73-89)	BOOK III
IV.	(Psalms 90-106)	BOOK IV
V.	(Psalms 107-150)	BOOK V

TYPES OF PSALMS:

NATIONAL PSALMS: 14, 44, 46-48, 53, 66, 68, 74, 76, 79, 80, 83, 87, 108, 122, 124-126, 129

HISTORICAL PSALMS: 78, 81, 105, 106, 144

MESSIANIC PSALMS: 2, 8, 16, 22, 24, 35, 40, 41, 68, 69 72, 87, 89, 97M 102 118, 132

REPENTANCE PSALMS: 6, 32, 38, 51, 102, 130, 143

IMPRECATORY PSALMS: 34, 52, 58, 69, 109, 137, 140

PRAISE PSALMS: 103, 106, 111-113, 117, 135, 146-150

THANKSGIVING PSALMS: 105, 107, 118, 136

HALLEL/PRAISE PSALMS SUNG
AT PASSOVER: 113-118

LAW PSALMS: 1, 19, 119

ACROSTIC PSALMS: 9, 10, 25, 34, 37, 111, 112, 119, 145

ASCENT PSALMS: 120-134

PROVERBS

I.	(1-9)	THE PRAISE OF WISDOM
II.	(10-24)	THE PROVERBS OF LIFE
III.	(25-29)	THE PRINCIPLES OF ORDER
IV.	(30-31)	THE PRAISE OF VIRTUE

Topic of Proverbs:

"The fear of the Lord"....1:29: 2:5; 3:7; 8:13; 9:10; 10:27;
14:26-27; 15:16, 33; 16:6; 19:23; 22:4; 23:17

ECCLESIASTES

I. (1:1-3) THE THEME OF "VANITY" IS PRESENTED

    A. (1:1)   THE WRITER PRESENTED
    B. (1:2-3) THE THEME PRESENTED

II. (1:4-3:22) THE THEME OF "VANITY" IS PROVED

    A. (1:4-11)   VANITY VIA THE CYCLE OF LIFE
    B. (1:12-18) VANITY VIA THE GRIEF OF WISDOM
    C. (2:1-12)   VANITY VIA THE FUTILITY OF MATERIALISM
    D. (2:13-26) VANITY VIA THE REALITY OF INHERITANCE
    E. (3:1-22)   VANITY VIA THE CERTAINTY OF DEATH

III. (4:1-12:8) THE THEME OF "VANITY" IS PROPAGATED

    A. (4)   VANITY VIA THE UNFAIR-NESS LIFE
    B. (5)   VANITY VIA THE FUTILITY OF WEALTH
    C. (6)   VANITY VIA HOPELESSNESS
    D. (7)   VANITY VIA THE REALITY OF MAN'S SIN
    E. (8-9)   VANITY VIA THE REALITY OF GOD'S PROVIDENCE

F.   (10)   VANITY VIA THE FOLLY OF LIFE

G.   (11:1-12:8) VANITY VIA THE GRIEF OF YOUTH AND OLD AGE

IV. (12:9-14) THE   THEME   OF "VANITY" IN PERSPECTIVE

A. (12:9-10)   THE PREACHER STILL TAUGHT AND SOUGHT

B. (12:11-12) THE WORDS OF WISDOM CAN BENEFIT

C. (12:13-14) THE CONCLUSION OF THE WHOLE MATTER

SONG OF SOLOMON

I.   (1)   THE BRIDE AND THE SHEPHERD

II.   (2)   THE PROMISE OF THE SHEPHERD

III.   (3)   THE RETURN OF THE SHEPHERD

IV.   (4)   THE SHEPHERD DESCRIBES THE BRIDE

V.   (5)   THE DREAM OF THE BRIDE

VI.   (6)   THE BEAUTY OF THE BRIDE IS PRAISED

VII. (7)   THE COMMUNION OF THE BRIDE AND THE SHEPHERD

VIII. (8)   THE RETURN BACK HOME

Isaiah

I.   (1-24)   BLESSING OUT OF JUDGMENT

   A. (1-12)   THE JUDGMENT OF ISRAEL
   B. (13-24) THE JUDGMENT OF THE NATIONS

II. (25-35) JUDGMENT OUOT OF BLESSING

   A. (25-27) THE PROCESS
   B. (28-33) THE PRONOUNCEMENT
   C. (34-35) THE PRODUCT

III. (36-39) THE HISTORY OF DELIVERANCE

   A. (36)   THE PROBLEM AT HAND
   B. (37)   THE SOLUTION FROM GOD'S HAND
   C. (38-39) PERSONAL VICTORY AND DEFEAT

IV. (40-48) THE COMFORT OF GOD

   A. (40-46) GOD'S HATRED OF IDOLATRY
   B. (47-48) GOD'S LOVE OF ISRAEL

V. (49-57)   THE SALVATION OF GOD

    A. (49-51)   SALVATION PROMISED
    B. (52-53)   SALVATION IN A PERSON
    C. (54-57)   SALVATION PROVISIONS

VI. (58-66)   THE GLORY OF GOD

    A. (58-63)   THE GLORY TO COME
    B. (64-66)   THE GLORY TO STAY

JEREMIAH

I. (1-45) JEREMIAH'S PROPHECY FOR JUDAH AND JERUSALEM

    A. (1)   JEREMIAH'S CALL
    B. (2-20)   JEREMIAH'S EIGHT MESSAGES OF SIN AND REPENTANCE
    C. (21-39)   JEREMIAH'S MESSAGES OF JUDGMENT AND BLESSING
    D. (40-45)   JEREMIAH'S MESSAGES TO THE JEWISH REMANANT

II. (46-51) JEREMIAH'S PROPHECY FOR THE NATIONS

A. (46)   EGYPT

B   (47)   PHILISTIA

C. (48)   MOAB

D. (49:1-6)   AMMON

E. (49:7-22)   EDOM

F. (49:23-27)   DAMASCUS

G. (49:28-33)   KEDAR AND HAZOR

H. (49:34-39)   ELAM

I. (50-51)   BABYLON

III. (52:1-34) JEREMIAH'S PROPHECY VINDICATED

A. (52:1-11)   JERUSALEM IS CAPTURED

B. (52:12-23)   JERUSALEM IS DESTROYED

C. (52:24-34)   JERUSALEM   CITIZENS   TAKEN
                 CAPTIVE

LAMENTATIONS

I. (1:1-22) JERUSALEM LAMENTS

A. (1:1-11)   JERUSALEM IS DEVASTATED

B. (1:12-22)   JERUSALEM WEEPS

II. (2:1-22)   THE HOLY PLACE LAMENTS

   A. (2:1-10)   THE REALITY OF GOD'S WRATH
   B. (2:11-22) THE RESPONSE TO GOD'S WRATH

III. (3:1-66)   JEREMIAH LAMENTS

   A. (3:1-18)   JEREMIAH'S SORROW OVER
                   SUFFERING
   B. (3:19-42) JEREMIAH'S PRAYER OF
                   REASSURANCE
   C. (3:43-66) JEREMIAH'S PRAYER FOR
                   VINDICATION

IV. (4:1-22)   THE JEWS LAMENT

   A. (4:1-11)   THE CARNAGE OF THE
                   CATASTROPHE
   B. (4:12-22) THE CAUSES OF THE
                   CATASTROPHE

V. (5:1-22)   LAMENTATIONS IN PERSPECTIVE

   A. (5:1-18)   UNDERSTANDING THE REASON
                   WHY
   B. (5:19-22) DESIRING A REVIVAL OF THE
                   WAY IT WAS

EZEKIEL

I. (1-3)   THE PROPHET EZEKIEL IS CALLED

   A. (1)   EZEKIEL'S VISION
   B. (2-3)   EZEKIEL'S CALL

II. (4-24)   EZEKIEL'S   PREDICTIONS   AGAINST
          ISRAEL

   A.   (4-7)   THE FOUR SIGNS OF COMING
               JUDGMENT
   B.   (8-11)   THE FOUR VISIONS OF COM-
               ING JUDGMENT
   C.   (12-19)   THE PARABLES OF COMING
               JUDGMENT
   D.   (20-24)   THE COMING JUDGMENT OF
               JERUSALEM

III. (24-32)   EZEKIEL'S   PREDICTIONS   AGAINST
           THE NATIONS

   A.   (25:1-7)   AMMON
   B.   (25:8-11)   MOAB
   C.   (25:12-14)   EDOM
   D.   (25:15-17)   PHILISTIA
   E.   (26-28:19)   TYRE
   F.   (28:20-26)   SIDON
   G.   (29-32)   EGYPT

IV. (33-39) EZEKIEL'S PREDICTIONS OF
RESTORATIONS

    A. (33) THE WATCHMAN
    B. (34) THE SHEPHERDS
    C. (35:1-36:7) THE SEQUENCE
    D. (36:8-38) THE RESTORATION
        EXPLAINED
    E. (37) THE RESTORATION
        ILLUSTRATED
    F. (38-39) THE BATTLE

V. (40-48) EZEKIEL'S PREDICTIONS OF THE
KINGDOM

    A. (40-43:12) THE TEMPLE OF THE
        KINGDOM
    B. (43:13-46:24) THE WORSHIP OF THE
        KINGDOM
    C. (47-48) THE LAND OF THE KINGDOM

DANIEL

I. (1-6) THE TIMELY EXPERIENCES OF DANIEL

    A. (1) THE TEST OF THE DIET
    B. (2) THE DREAM OF THE IMAGE

C. (3)   THE FIERY FURNACE
D. (4)   THE DREAM OF THE TREE
E. (5)   THE HANDWRITING ON THE WALL
F. (6)   THE LION'S DEN

II. (7-12)   THE TIMELY VISIONS OF DANIEL

A. (7)   THE FOUR BEASTS
B. (8)   THE TWO BEASTS
C. (9)   THE SEVENTY WEEKS PROPHECY
D. (10-12) ANGELIC WAR/MAN OF SIN/ TRIBULATION DAYS

Hosea

I. (1-3) GOMER, THE ADULTEROUS WIFE

    A. (1)   THE MARRIAGE OF HOSEA AND GOMER

    B. (2)   THE MARRIAGE OF GOD AND ISRAEL

    C. (3)   THE ADULTEROUS ONE RESTORED

II. (4-14) ISRAEL, THE ADULTEROUS NATION

    A. (4-5)   THE RECORD OF THE NATION

    B. (6-9)   THE RESPONSE OF GOD

    C. (10-11)   THE REMEMBRANCE OF THE PAST

    D. (12-13:8) THE RECOMPENSE TO THE NATION

    E. (13:9-14:9) THE RESTORATION OF ISRAEL UNTO GOD

JOEL

I. (1) THE PLAGUE OF LOCUST DESCRIBED

    A. (1:1-4)   THE SCOPE OF THE PLAGUE
    B. (1:5-13)   THE RESULT OF THE PLAGUE
    C. (1:14-15) THE REACTION OF THE PRIESTS
    D. (1:16-20) THE PLIGHT UPON THE ANIMALS

II. (2-3) THE PLAGUE OF LOCUSTS DETERMINED

    A. (2:1-12)   DETERMINED TO MEAN AN
                    INVASION TO COME
    B. (2:13-17) DETERMINED TO MEAN THE
                    REPENTANCE OF THE PEOPLE
    C. (2:18-32) DETERMINED TO MEAN THE
                    DELIVERANCE OF GOD
    D. (3:1-16)   DETERMINED TO MEAN THE
                    JUDGMENT OF THE NATIONS
    E. (3:17-21) DETERMINED TO MEAN THE
                    BLESSING OF THE KINGDOM

AMOS

I. (1:1-2:16) THE TRANSGRESSORS TO BE JUDGED

    A. (1:1-5)   DAMASCUS
    B. (1:6-8)   GAZA

C. (1:9-10) TYRE
D. (1:11-12) EDOM
E. (1:13-15) AMMON
F. (2:1-3) MOAB
G. (2:4-5) JUDAD
H. (2:6-16) ISRAEL

II (3:1-6:14) THE TRANSGRESSORS' SINS

A. (3:1-15) PRIVILEGES MISUSED
B. (4:1-5) WORSHIP MISGUIDED
C. (4:6-13) WARNINGS MISUNDERSTOOD
D. (5:1-27) WEEPING OVER ISRAEL
E. (6:1-14) WOE ON ISRAEL

III. (7:1-9:10) THE TRANSGRESSORS WANTED

A. (7:1-3) THE GRASSHOPPERS
B. (7:4-6) THE FIRE
C. (7:7-9) THE PLUMB LINE
D. (7:10-17) AMAZIAH
E. (8:1-14) THE SUMMER FRUIT
F. (9:1-10) THE LINTEL

IV. (9:11-15) THE KINGDOM TO COME

A. (9:11) THE KINGDOM GOVERNMENT
B. (9:12) THE KINGDOM PEOPLE
C. (9:13) THE KINGDOM BLESSING

D. (9:14) THE KINGDOM PEACE
E. (9:15) THE KINGDOM'S DURATION

OBADIAH

I. (1-9) THE JUDGMENT OF EDOM IS PRO-
NOUNCED
II. (10-14) THE JUDGMENT OF EDOM IS DE-
FENDED
III. (15-21) THE JUDGMENT OF ESAU AND THE
ESTABLISHMENT OF JERUSALEM

JONAH

I. (1) JONAH PURSUED BY THE LORD
II. (2) JONAH PRAYING UNTO THE LORD
III. (3) JONAH PREACHING FOR THE LORD
IV. (4) JONAH POUTING BEFORE THE LORD

MICAH

I. (1-3) GOD ALONE IS JUDGE

A. (1:1-7) JUDGMENT ANNOUNCED

B. (1:8-16) JUDGMENT ON THE CITIES
C. (2:1-11) JUDGMENT'S INDICTMENT
D. (2:12-13) JUDGMENT'S ADMINISTERING
E. (3:1-12) JUDGMENT DENOUNCED

II. (4-5) GOD ALONE IS DELIVERED

A. (4:1-8) THE BLESSING OF DELIVERANCE
B. (4:9-5:1) THE NEED FOR DELIVERANCE
C. (5:2-9) THE PERSON OF DELIVERANCE
D. (5:10-15) THE EXECUTION OF DELIVERANCE

III. (6-7) GOD ALONE IS RIGHTEOUS

A. (6:1-8) GOD'S RIGHTEOUSNESS BASED ON REPENTANCE
B. (6:9-16) GOD'S RIGHTEOUSNESS IS REASON FOR JUDGMENT
C. (7:1-6) GOD'S RIGHTEOUSNESS CONTRASTED WITH MAN'S
D. (7:7-20) GOD'S RIGHTEOUSNESS IS UNIQUE TO HIM

NAHUM

I. (1) NAHUM FORETELLS THE DOM OF NINEVEH

A. (1:1-7) THE GOD OF JUDGMENT
DESCRIBED
B. (1:8-15) THE JUDGMENT OF GOD
DESCRIBED

II. (2) NAHUM DESCRIBES THE DOOM OF
NINEVEH

A. (2:1-8) NINEVEH IS CAPTURED
B. (2:9-13) NINEVEH IS SPOILED

III. (3) NAHUM DECLARES THE DESERVED
DOOM OF NINEVEH

A. (3:1-3) THEIR GUILT OF BLOODSHED
B. (3:4-7) THEIR GUILT OF IDOLATRY
C. (3:8-19) THEIR GUILT OF PRIDE

HABAKKUK

I.   (1:1-2:1) HABAKKUK'S QUESTIONING OF
GOD
II. (2:2-20) GOD'S ANSWERING OF HABAK-
KUK
III. (3) HABAKKUK'S DOXOLOGY OF
FAITH

ZEPHANIAH

I. (1:1-3:7) TRIBULATION IN THE DAY OF THE
LORD

   A. (1:1-2:3) JUDAH IN THE DAY OF THE LORD
   B. (2:4-15) THE NATIONS IN THE DAY OF THE
LORD
   C. (3:1-7) GOD IN THE DAY OF THE LORD

II. (3:8-20) TRIUMPH IN THE DAY OF THE LORD

   A. (3:8-13) THE REMNANT OF THE DAY
OF THE LORD
   B. (3:14-17) THE KING OF THE DAY OF
THE LORD
   C. (3:18-20) THE REGATHERING OF THE
DAY OF THE LORD

HAGGAI

I. (1:1-11) HAGGAI'S REBUKE OF THE JEWS
II. (1:12-15) HAGGAI'S PROMISE TO THE
JEWS
III. (2:1-9) HAGGAI'S ENCOURAGEMENT TO
THE JEWS

ZECHARIAH

C. (8:1-17) THE MESSAGE OF EXPECTATION
D. (8:18-23) THE MESSAGE OF EXALTATION

III. (9:1-14:21) ISRAEL'S FUTURE SEEN IN THE TWO BURDENS

    A. (9-11) THE BURDEN UPON THE NATIONS
    B. (12-14) THE BURDEN UPON ISRAEL

MALACHI

I. (1:1-5) THE DECLARATION OF GOD'S LOVE

II. (1:6-2:9) THE DECLARATION OF THE PEOPLE'S IGNORANCE

III. (2:10-16) THE DECLARATION OF THE PEOPLE'S DISOBEDIENCE

IV. (2:17-3:6) THE DECLARATION OF GOD'S JUDGMENT TO COME

V. (3:7-12) THE DECLARATION OF THE PEOPLE ROBBING GOD

VI. (3:13-4:6) THE DECLARATION OF GOD'S FUTURE BLESSING

BETWEEN THE TESTAMENTS

The four centuries between the Old and New Testaments have been called the "Silent Years" because of the absence of God's revelation to the world through the Jews. This was a dark period in Israel's history when neither prophet nor inspired writer could be found. From the time of Nehemiah to the time of John the Baptist, history progressed without any direct revelation from God. But, God, nevertheless, was in control as He moved upon men and nations to prepare the way for His son, Jesus Christ.

The seat of political power passed from the East to the West, from Asia to Europe. The Persian empire fell under the strong arm of the Macedonians and the Greek empire in turn was conquered by the roman rulers. Thus, the Christ would be born into a world with one government and one predominant language. The Jews were a nation without a country and the spiritual condition of the world cried for God's help in the face of religiosity, idolatry, immorality, and paganism. Indeed, the fullness of time had come (Gal. 4:4-5)!

Matthew

I. (1-10)   THE PRESENTATION OF THE KINGDOM

   A. (1-4)   THE PRESON OF THE KING
   B. (5-7)   THE PREACHING OF THE KING
   C. (8-10) THE POWER OF THE KING

II. (11-23)   THE REBELLION AGAINST THE
              KINGDOM

   A. (11-12)   THE DECLARATIONS OF THE
                   REBELLION
   B. (13)   THE CONSEQUENCES OF
                   THE REBELLION
   C. (14-22:14)   THE DEVELOPMENT OF THE
                   REBELLION
   D. (22:5-23:39) THE RELIGIOUS ASPECT OF
                   THE REBELLION

III. (24-25)   THE ANTICIPATION OF THE KINGDOM

   A. (24:1-3)   THE SETTING

B.   (24:4-31)   THE TEACHING
C.   (24:32-25:46) THE PARABLES

IV. (26-28)   THE REJECTION OF THE KINGDOM

A.   (26-27)   THE KING IS CRUCIFIED
B.   (28:1-15)   THE KING IS RESURRECTED
C.   (28:16-20) THE KING COMMISSIONS HIS
                       SUBJECTS

MARK

I.   (1:1-8:26)   THE SERVANT CAME TO SERVE

A.   (1:1-2:12)   THE MESSAGES AND
                     MIRACLES
B.   (2:13-3:12)   THE DISTRUST AND DENIALS
C.   (3:13-19)   THE SERVANT AND HIS
                     SERVANTS
D.   (3:20-35)   THE SERVANT AND THE
                     SELF-RIGHTEOUS

1.   (4:1-5:43)   THE MESSAGES AND MIRACLES
2.   (6:1-6)   THE DISTRUST AND DENIALS
3.   (6:7-56)   THE SERVANT AND HIS
                     SERVANTS
4.   (7:1-8:26)   THE SERVANT AND THE
                     SELF-RIGHTEOUS

II. (8:27-16:20)   THE SERVANT CAME TO DIE

    A. (8:27-9:32)   THE SERVANT'S PERSON
    B. (9:33-10:52) THE SERVANT'S PRINCIPLES
    C. (11:1-13:37) THE SERVANT'S
                    PROCLAMATION

      1. (14:1-42)   THE SERVANT PREPARES TO
                          DIE
      2. (14:43-15:15) THE SERVANT ON TRIAL
      3. (15:16-47)   THE SERVANT IS CRUCIFIED
      4. (16:1-20)   THE SERVANT IS
                          RESURRECTED AND
                          ASCENDS

LUKE

I. (1-3) THE SON OF MAN'S BIRTH AND CHILDHOOD

    A. (1)   THE BIRTH AND GROWTH OF
              JOHN THE BAPTIST
    B. (2)   THE BIRTH AND GROWTH OF JESUS
    C. (3)   THE BAPTISM OF JESUS BY JOHN
              THE BAPTIST

II. (4:1-13)   THE SON OF MAN'S TEMPTATION BY
               THE DEVIL

    A. (4:1-4)   THE FIRST TEMPTATION

JOHN

I. (1:1-12:50) THE SON OF GOD BEFORE THE WORLD

    A. (1) THE SON OF GOD AND HIS PERSON

    B. (2-5) THE SON OF GOD AND HIS MESSAGE TO INDIVIDUALS

    C. (6-10) THE SON OF GOD AND HIS MESSAGE TO GROUPS

    D. (11-12) THE SON OF GOD IS RECEIVED

II. (13-17) THE SON OF GOD AMONG HIS DISCIPLES

    A. (13) THE SON OF GOD GIVES THE EXAMPLE

    B. (14) THE SON OF GOD GIVES THE COMFORTER

    C. (15) THE SON OF GOD GIVES ABUNDANT LIFE

    D. (16) THE SON OF GOD GIVES SPIRITUAL TRUTH

    E. (17) THE SON OF GOD GIVES "THE LORD'S PRAYER"

III. (18-19) THE SON OF GOD ON THE CROSS

    A. (18:1-11) THE SON OF GOD IN THE GARDEN

C. (3-5)   THE WITNESS OF THE EARLY
             CHURCH
D. (6-7)   THE WITNESS OF THE FIRST MARTYR
             OF THE CHURCH

II. (8-12)   WITNESSING TO JEDEA AND SAMARIA

   A. (8)   THE SCATTERING OF THE
                   WITNESSES
   B. (9)   THE WITNESS TO SAUL OF
                   THE ROAD TO DAMASCUS
   C. (10-11:18) THE WITNESS OF PETER TO
                   THE GENTILES
   D. (11:19-3)   THE WITNESS OF THE
                   CHURCH AT ANTIOCH
   E. (12)   THE WITNESS OF THE DEATH
                   OF JAMES AND HEROD

III. (13-28) WITNESSING TO THE UTTERMOST
              PART OF THE WORLD

   A. (13-14)   THE FIRST MISSIONARY
                      JOURNEY
   B. (15:1-35)   THE JERUSALEM COUNCIL
   C. (15:36-18:22) THE SECOND MISSIONARY
                      JOURNEY
   D. (18:23021:17) THE THIRD MISSIONARY
                      JOURNEY
   E. (21:18-26:32) THE WITNESS OF PAUL IN
                      JERUSALEM
   F. (27-28)   THE WITNESS OF PAUL IN ROME

Romans

I. (1-3:20) THE RIGHTEOUSNESS OF GOD NEEDED

   A. (1:1-32) THE GENTILES ARE IN NEED
   B. (2:1-3:8) THE JEWS ARE IN NEED
   C. (3:9-20) ALL ARE IN NEED

II. (3:21-4:25) THE RIGHTEOUSNESS OF GOD PROVIDED

   A. (3:21-26) PROVISION THROUGH THE DEATH OF CHRIST
   B. (3:27-4:25) PROVISION THROUGH THE EXERCISING OF FAITH

III. (5:1-8:39) THE RIGHTEOUSNESS OF GOD EFFECTIVE

   A. (5:1-21) THE EFFECTIVE BLESSING OF CHRIST
   B. (6:1-7:25) THE EFFECTIVE FREEDOM OF CHRIST

C. (8:1-27) THE EFFECTIVE SPIRIT OF CHRIST

D. (8:28-39) THE EFFECTIVE UNION WITH CHRIST

IV. (9-11) THE RIGHTEOUSNESS OF GOD DEFENDED

    A. (9) DEFENDED FROM ISRAEL'S PAST

    B. (10) DEFENDED FROM ISRAEL'S PRESENT

    C. (11) DEFENDED FROM ISRAEL'S FUTURE

V. (12-16) THE RIGHTEOUSNESS OF GOD APPLIED

    A. (12:1-8) THE APPLICATION BETWEEN GOD AND THE BELIEVER

    B. (12:9-16) THE APPLICATION BETWEEN BELIEVERS

    C. (12:17-21) THE APPLICATION BETWEEN BELIEVERS AND UNBELIEVERS

    D. (13:1-7) THE APPLICATION BETWEEN BELIEVERS AND GOVERNMENTS

    E. (13:8-14) THE APPLICATION BETWEEN BELIEVERS AND THE LAW OF LOVE

    F. (14:1-15:13) THE APPLICATION BETWEEN THE BELIEVER AND HIS ACTIONS

I CORINTHIANS

C. (11)   DIFFICULTIES OVER THE LORD'S
              SUPPER
D. (12-14)   DIFFICULTIES ABOUT SPIRITUAL
              GIFTS

IV. (15-16) DOCTRINE   WITHIN   THE   LOCAL
            CHURCH

    A. (15:1-11)   THE DOCTRINE OF THE GOSPEL
    B. (15:12-58) THE DOCTRINE OF THE
                          RESURRECTION
    C. (16:1-24)   THE DOCTRINE OF GIVING AND
                          PERSONAL GREETINGS

II CORINTHIANS

I. (1-7)   PAUL'S EXPLANATION OF HIS INISTRY

    A. (1-2) HIS TRIUMPHANT MINISTRY
    B. (3)   HIS GLORIOUS MINISTRY
    C. (4)   HIS HONEST MINISTRY
    D. (5)   HIS AMBITIOUS MINISTRY
    E. (6-7) HIS LOVING MINISTRY

II. (8-9)   PAUL'S EXHORTATION TO THE PEOPLE

    A. (8)   THE PRINCIPLES OF GIVING
    B. (9)   THE PROMISES TO GIVERS

III. (10-13)   PAUL   EXPOUNDS   HIS   APOSTOLIC
AUTHORITY

   A.   (10)   THE APOSTLE AS A SOLDIER
   B.   (11:1-15)   THE APOSTLE AS A FATHER
   C.   (11:16-12:10)   THE APOSTLE AS AN EX-
                           AMPLE
   D.   (12:11-13:14)   THE APOSTLE AS A LEADER
                           GALATIANS

I.   (1-2)   THE VINDICATION OF THE TRUE GOSPEL

   A.   (1:1-24)   THE   GOSPEL   MESSAGE   IS   FROM
                       GOD
   B.   (2:1-10)   THE GOSPEL MISSION IS FROM GOD
   C.   (2:11-21) THE GOSPEL MANNER IS FROM GOD

II. (3-4) THE EXPLANATION OF THE TRUE GOSPEL

   A.   (3:1-14)   THE GOSPEL EXPLAINED BY
                       EXAMPLE
   B.   (3:15-22) THE GOSPEL EXPLAINED BY
                       CONTRAST
   C.   (3:23-4:7) THE GOSPEL EXPLAINED BY
                       ANALOGY
   D.   (4:8-20)   THE GOSPEL EXPLAINED BY
                       DESIRE
   E.   (4:21-31) THE GOSPEL EXPLAINED BY
                       ALLEGORY

III. (5-6) THE APPLICATION OF THE TRUE GOSPEL

    A. (5:1) THE FREEDOM OF THE GOSPEL PRESENTED

    B. (5:2-12) THE HINDERANCE OF THE GOSPEL REBUKED

    C. (5:13-15) THE USE OF THE GOSPEL'S FREEDOM OUTLINED

    D. (5:16-24) THE BATTLING OF THE GOSPEL'S FREEDOM DESCRIBED

    E. (5:25-6:18) THE FRUIT OF THE GOSPEL'S FREEDOM REVEALED

EPHESIANS

I. (1-3) THE BELIEVER "IN CHRIST" IN THE HEAVENLIES

    A. (1:1-14) THE BELIEVER AND THE WORK OF THE TRINITY

    B. (1:15-2:10) THE BELIEVER MADE SPIRITUALLY ALIVE IN CHRIST

    C. (2:11-22) THE BELIEVER IN THE BODY OF CHRIST

    D. (3:1-21) THE BELIEVER AND THE MYSTERY OF THE CHURCH

II. (4-6) THE BELIEVER "IN CHRIST" IN THE WORLD

A. (4:1-16)   WALKING IN UNITY
B. (4:17-29)   WALKING IN SEPARATION
C. (4:30-5:20) WALKING IN THE SPIRIT
D. (5:21-6:9   WALKING IN RESPECT TO ONE ANOTHER
E. (6:10-24)   WALKING IN THE MIDST OF A SPIRITUAL BATTLE

PHILIPPIANS

I. (1) THE MEANING OF LIFE

A. (1:1-11)   THE CONFIDENCE IN CHRIST
B. (1:12-19) THE CONTENTMENT IN CHRIST
C. (1:20-30) THE COMMITMENT IN CHRIST

II. (2) THE MOTIVATION OF LIFE

A. (2:1-11)   CHRIST, OUR PERFECT EXAMPLE
B. (2:12-16) CHRISTIANS, OUR PRESENT EXAMPLE
C. (2:17-30) CHRISTIAN LEADERS, OUR PERSONAL EXAMPLES

III. (3)   THE MANDATE OF LIFE

    A.   (3:1-11)   TO KNOW OF CHRIST
    B.   (3:12-19) TO LOOK TO CHRIST
    C.   (3:20-21) TO LOOK FOR CHRIST

IV. (4)   THE MANIFESTATIONS OF LIFE

    A.   (4:1-4)   UNITY OF THE BRETHREN
    B.   (4:5-7)   PEACE WITH THE LORD
    C.   (4:8-9)   THE VIRTUOUS THOUGHT LIFE
    D.   (4:10-12) CONTENTMENT WITH LOT IN
                   LIFE
    E.   (4:13-23) TRUSTING IN THE LORD

COLOSSIANS

I.   (1:1-2:19)   THE PERSON OF CHRIST

    A.   (1:1-23)   CHRIST IN THE PRAYER OF PAUL
    B.   (1:24-2:5) CHRIST IN THE MINISTRY OF PAUL
    C.   (2:6-19)   CHRIST IN THE DOCTRINE OF PAUL

II. (2:20-4:18)   THE PERSONS OF CHRISTIANITY

    A.   (2:20-3:4)   CHRISTIAN UNIQUENESS
    B.   (3:5-17)   CHRISTIAN LIVING
    C.   (3:18-21)   CHRISTIAN FAMILY

I THESSALONIANS

C. (5:1-22)   THE BELIEVER'S WORK OF DO-ING THE LORD'S WILL

D. (5:23-28)   THE PRAYER FOR THE THESSA-LONIANS

II THESSALONIANS

I. (1:1-12)   THANKSGIVING AND ENCOURAGEMENT IN PERSECUTION

    A. (1:3-4)   COMMENDATION FOR SPIRITUAL GROWTH

    B. (1:5-6)   EXPLANATION OF PERSECUTION

    C. (1:7-10)   REVELATION OF CHRIST THE RIGHTEOUS JUDGE

    D. (1:11-12)   INTERCESSION FOR CONTINUED SPIRITUAL GROWTH

II. (2:1-17)   CORRECTION CONCERNING THE DAY OF THE LORD

    A. (2:1-2)   IN REGARD TO THE PRESENT

    B. (2:3a)   IN REGARD TO THE APOSTASY

    C. (2:3b-5)   IN REGARD TO THE ANTI-CHRIST

    D. (2:6-9)   IN REGARD TO THE RESTRAINER

    E. (2:10-12)   IN REGARD TO THE UNBELIEVERS

    F. (2:13-17)   IN REGARD TO THE BELIEVERS

III. (3:1-15)   EXHORTATION   TO   PRAYER   AND
                DISCIPLINE

   A.   (3:1-2)   THE REQUEST FOR PRAYER
   B.   (3:3-5)   THE REMINDER OF GOD'S
                   FAITHFULNESS
   C.   (3:6-15)   THE APOSTLE PAUL'S COM-
                   MANDS

I TIMOTHY

I. (1:1-3:16)   PAUL'S EXHORTATION AND
                 CHARGE TO A YOUNG CHURCH

   A. (1:1-20) MAINTAIN INTEGRITY OF DOCTRINE
   B. (2:1-15) MAINTAIN INTEGRITY OF BEHAVIOR
   C. (3:1-16) MAINTAIN INTEGRITY OF LEADERS

II. (4:1-6:21)   PAUL'S EXHORTATION AND CHARGE
                 TO A YOUNG PASTOR

   A.   (4:1-16)   MAINTAIN PURITY OF DOCTRINE
   B.   (5:1-6:2)   MAINTAIN PURITY OF CHURCH
                  LEADERSHIP
   C.   (6:3-21)   MAINTAIN PURITY OF PERSONAL
                  TESTIMONY

II TIMOTHY

I. (1:1-18)   THE PRAISE OF TIMOTHY'S PAST

    A. (1:1-5)   TIMOTHY'S GODLY HERITAGE
    B. (1:6-7)   TIMOTHY'S GIFT FROM GOD
    C. (1:8-14)   TIMOTHY'S FAITHFUL GOD
    D. (1:15-18) TIMOTHY IN CONTRAST TO OTHERS

II. (2:1-26)   THE PATTERNS OF TIMOTHY'S PRESENT

    A. (2:1-2)   BE A TEACHER
    B. (2:3-4)   BE A SOLDIER
    C. (2:5)   BE AN ATHLETE
    D. (2:6)   BE A FARMER
    E. (2:7-13)   BE ONE WHO UNDERSTANDS
    F. (2:14-15) BE A WORKMAN
    G. (2:16-19) BE ONE WHO DISCERNS
    H. (2:20-23) BE A VESSEL OF HONOR
    I. (2:24-26) BE A SERVANT

III. (3:1-4:5)   THE PRECAUTIONS OF TIMOTHY'S FUTURE

    A. (3:1-9)   THE TIMES
    B. (3:10-12) THE CONTRAST
    C. (3:13-14) THE DOCTRINE

D. (3:15-17) THE SCRIPTURES
E. (4:1-5)   THE PREACHING

IV. (4:6-22)   THE PERSONAL MATTERS AT HAND

    A. (4:6-8)   PAUL'S PERSONAL TESTIMONY
    B. (4:9-18)   PAUL'S PERSONAL DESIRES
    C. (4:19-22) PAUL'S PERSONAL SALUTATION

TITUS

I. (1:1-16) RIGHTEOUS LIVING WITHIN THE CHURCH

    A. (1:1-9)   TRUE LEADERS DESCRIBED
    B. (1:10-12) FALSE LEADERS DESCRIBED
    C. (1:13-16) UNBELIEVERS DESCRIBED

II. (2:1-15) RIGHTEOUS LIVING WITHIN THE HOME

    A. (2:1-6)   PROPER FAMILY LIFE
    B. (2:7-8)   PROPER EXAMPLE OF TITUS
    C. (2:9-10)   PROPER WORKING RELATIONS
    D. (2:11-15) PROPER SPIRITUAL PERSPECTIVE

III. (3:1-15)   RIGHTEOUS LIVING WITHIN THE
                WORLD

    A.   (3:1-3)   OBEYING THOSE IN AUTHORITY
    B.   (3:4-7)   OBEYING GOD IN SALVATION
    C.   (3:8-15) OBEYING GOD IN SANCTIFICATION
                             AND PERSONAL GREETINGS

PHILEMON

I.   (1-3)   PAUL GREETS PHILEMON
II.   (4-7)   PAUL COMMENDS PHILEMON
III. (8-20)   PAUL REQUESTS OF PHILEMON
IV.   (21-22)   PAUL'S CONFIDENCE IN PHILEMON
V.   (23-25)   PAUL'S BENEDICTION

HEBREWS

I.   (1-7)   THE PERSON OF CHRIST IS "BETTER"

    A.   (1:1-3)   CHRIST IS GOD
    B.   (1:4-2:18) CHRIST IS BETTER THAN THE
                            ANGELS
    C.   (3:1-19)   CHRIST IS BETTER THAN MOSES
    D.   (4:1-13)   CHRIST IS BETTER THAN JOSHUA

E. (4:14-7:7) CHRIST IS BETTER THAN ABRAHAM

F. (7:8-28) CHRIST IS BETTER THAN LEVI

II. (8:1-10:18) THE PERFORMANCE OF CHRIST IS "BETTER"

A. (8:1-13) BECAUSE OF THE NEW COVENANT

B. (9:1-11) BECAUSE OF THE HEAVENLY SANCTUARY

C. (9:12-28) BECAUSE OF THE BLOOD OF CHRIST

D. (10:1-18) BECAUSE OF THE FINISHED WORK OF CHRIST

III. (10:19-13:25) THE PROVISION OF CHRIST IS "BETTER"

A. (10:19-39) CHRIST PROVIDES FULL ASSURANCE

B. (11:1-40) CHRIST PROVIDES FULL FAITH

C. (12:1-11) CHRIST PROVIDES LOVING CHASTISEMENT

D. (12:12-29) CHRIST PROVIDES PERFECT MEDIATION

E. (13:1-25) CHRIST PROVIDES INSTRUCTIONS FOR CHRISTIAN LIVING

James

I.. (1:1-27). OUR FAITH IS PROVED TO OURSELVES

    A.   (1:1-8)   THROUGH TRAILS
    B.   (1:9-11)   THROUGH STATUS
    C.   (1:12-18) THROUGH TEMPTATIONS
    D.   (1:19-27) THROUGH ACTIONS

II. (2:1-26)   OUR FAITH IS PROVED TO OTHERS

    A.   (2:1-13)   BY BEING IMPARTIAL WITH OTHERS
    B.   (2:14-26) BY BEING CHARITABLE

III. (3:1-4:17) OUR FAITH IS PROVED TO THE WORLD

    A.   (3:1-12)   IN REGARD TO SPEECH
    B.   (3:13-18) IN REGARD TO WISDOM
    C.   (4:1-10)   IN REGARD TO WORLDLINESS
    D.   (4:11-12) IN REGARD TO PASSING JUDGMENT
    E.   (4:13-17) IN REGARD TO WILL OF GOD

IV. (5:1-20) OUR FAITH IS PROVED TO THE LORD

    A. (5:1-11)   VIA OOUR PATIENT SERVICE
    B. (5:12)   VIA OUR SINCERE SERVICE
    C. (5:13-18) VIA OUR PRAYERFUL SERVICE
    D. (5:19-20) VIA OUR HELPFUL SERVICE

I PETER

I. (1:1-12)   THE SALVATION OF GOD

    A. (1:1-5)   OUR LIVING HOPE
    B. (1:6-9)   OUR LIVING JOY
    C. (1:10-12) OUR LIVING REDEMPTION

II. (1:13-2:12) THE SANCTIFICATION OF GOD

    A. (1:13-17) THE FATHER'S HOLY CALL
    B. (1:18-22) THE SON'S PRECIOUS BLOOD
    C. (1:23-2:4) THE WORD'S LIVING POWER
    D. (2:5-12)   THE BELIEVER'S POSITION

III. (2:13-3:12)   THE SUBJECTION OF THE GODLY

    A. (2:13-20)   THE PRINCIPLE OF
                       SUBJECTION ESTABLISHED

B. (2:21-25)   THE PRINCIPLE OF
                SUBJECTION ILLUSTRATED
C   (3:1-12)   THE PRINCIPLE OF
                SUBJECTION APPLIED

IV. (3:13-5:14)   THE SUFFERING OF THE GODLY

A. (3:13-4:1)   SUFFERING FOR
                 RIGHTEOUSNESS' SAKE
B. (4:2-6)   SUFFERING WAS PREFIGURED
                 IN CHRIST
C. (4:7-13)   SUFFERING SHOULD NOT
                 CANCEL OUR COMMITMENT
D. (4:14-19)   SUFFERING HAS VARIOUS
                 CAUSES
E. (5:1-14)   SUFFERING SHOULD
                 PRODUCE HUMILITY AND
                 STEADFASTNESS

II PETER

I. (1:1-21)   THE DEVELOPMENT OF FAITH

A. (1:3-4)   POWER AND PROMISES
B. (1;5-11)   CONFIRMATION OF CHRISTLIKENESS
C. (1:12-21) PETER REMINDS HIS READERS

II. (2:1-22) THE DENOUNCING OF FALSE
TEACHERS

    A. (2:1-3) FOLLOWERS OF FALSE TEACHERS
    B. (2:4-8) FIGURESFROMTHEOLDTESTAMENT
              ABOUT FALSE TEACHERS
    C. (2:9-14) FUTURE OF THE FALSE TEACHERS
    D. (2:15-22) FEATURES OF FALSE TEACHERS

III. (3:1-18) THE DESIGN OF THE FUTURE

    A. (3:1-7) THE DISBELIEF
    B. (3:8-9) THE DELAY
    C. (3:10-13) THE DESTRUCTION
    D. (3:14-18) THE DILIGENCE

I JOHN

I. (1:1-2:29) FELLOWSHIP AND ITS
MAINTENANCE

    A. (1:1-4) FELLOWSHIP BASED ON THE
              LORD
    B. (1:5-7) FELLOWSHIP BASED ON THE
              LIGHT

C. (1:8-2:2) FELLOWSHIP BASED ON THE LOVING FORGIVENESS OF CHRIST

D. (2:3-29) FELLOWSHIP BASED ON LOVING THE BRETHREN, NOT THE WORLD

II. (3:1-4:21) FELLOWSHIP AND ITS MANIFESTATION

A. (3:1-10) PRACTICING RIGHTEOUSNESS
B. (3:11-24) LOVING THE BRETHREN
C. (4:1-6) DISCERNING THE SPIRITS
D. (4:7-21) UNDERSTANDING TRUE LOVE

III. (5:1-21) FELLOWSHIP AND ITS PRIVILEGES

A. (5:1-12) THE PRIVILEGE OF OVERCOMING THE WORLD
B. (5:13) THE PRIVILEGE OF ASSURANCE OF ETERNAL LIFE
C. (5:14-17) THE PRIVILEGE OF ANSWERED PRAYER
D. (5:18-19) THE PRIVILEGE OF VICTORY OVER SIN
E. (5:20-21) THE PRIVILEGE OF OUR LORD WHO UNDERSTANDS

II JOHN

I.   (1-3)   THE SALUTATION TO THE ELECT LADY
II. (4-6)   THE COMMENDATION OF THE CHURCH
III. (7-11) THE EXHORTATION ABOUT DECEIVERS
IV. (12-13) THE BENEDICTION

III JOHN

I.   (1-8)   GAIUS
II. (9-11) DIOTREPHES
III. (12-14) DEMETRIUS

JUDE

I.   (1-4)   THE SALUTATION

    A.   (1-2)   THE GREETING
    B.   (3-4)   THE PURPOSE

II. (5-19)   THE JUDGMENT OF APOSTASY

    A.   (5-7)   THE HISTORY OF APOSTASY
    B.   (8-16)   THE DESCRIPTION OF APOSTATES
    C.   (17-19) THE WARNING OF APOSTASY

III. (20-23)   THE SAFEGUARD AGAINST APOSTASY

    A.   (20-21)   IN REGARD TO SELF
    B.   (22-23)   IN REGARD TO OTHERS

IV. (24-25) THE BENEDICTION

    A.   (24)   GOD'S POWER
    B.   (25)   GOD'S PERSON

REVELATION

I.   (1:1-19)   THE THINGS HE HAS SEEN

    A.   (1:1-3)   TITLE AND BLESSING GIVEN
    B.   (1:4-8)   GREETING   AND   DESCRIPTION
             GIVEN
    C.   (1:9-19) VISION RECEIVED AND COMMAND
             GIVEN

II.   (1:20-3:22)   THE THINGS WHICH ARE

    A.   (1:20-2:7)   EPHESUS
    B.   (2:8-11)   SMYRNA
    C.   (2:12-17)   PERGAMOS
    D.   (2:18-29)   THYATIRA
    E.   (3:1-6)   SARDIS

F.   (3:7-13)   PHILADELPHIA
G.   (3:14-22)   LAODICEA

III. (4:1-22:7)   THINGS WHICH SHALL BE AFTER THIS

A. (4-5)   THE THRONE ROOM IN HEAVEN
B. (6)   THE SIX SEAL JUDGMENTS
C. (7)   THE TWO MULTITUDES
D. (8-9)   THE SIX TRUMPET JUDGMENTS
E. (10:1-11:13) THE TWO VISIONS
F. (11:14-19) THE SEVENTH TRUMPET JUDGMENT
G. (12-13)   THE PEOPLE OF THE TIMES
H. (14)   THE WORDS OF THE ANGELS
I. (15-16)   THE SEVEN BOWL JUDGMENTS
J. (17-18)   BABYLON
K. (19)   THE RETURN OF CHRIST TO THE EARTH
L. (20:1-10)   THE KINGDOM
M. (20:11-15) THE GREAT WHITE THRONE JUDGMENT
N. (21-22:7) THE NEW THINGS

IV. (22:8-21) THE LAST WORDS OF THE ANGEL, CHRIST, AND JOHN

Appendix I

Key Verses/Words For Each Bible Book

GENESIS 1:1, 26-27; 12:1   **(Beginning)**

EXODUS 3:8; 12:51   **(Passover)**

LEVITICUS 19:2   **(Atonement)**

NUMBERS 10:9; 29   **(Sojourn)**

DEUTERONOMY 4:23; 5:29   **(Obedience)**

JOSHUA 1:8; 11:23   **(Possession)**

JUDGES 2:19; 17:6   **(Anarchy)**

RUTH 1:9; 4:22   **(Kinsman-Redeemer)**

I SAMUEL 11:15   **(Kingdom)**

II SAMUEL 5:4   **(Covenant)**

I KINGS 9:4-5   **(Royalty)**

II KINGS 17:18-19; 23:27   **(Divided)**

I CHRONICLES 29:12   **(Theocracy)**

II CHRONICLES 1:1; 20:20b   **(Wisdom)**

EZRA 2:1; 6:21-22; 7:10   **(Restore)**

NEHEMIAH 2:17b; 6:3   **(Rebuild)**

ESTHER 4:14b	(Providence)
JOB 23:10	(Trials)
PSALMS 1; 23; 90; 119; 139; 15	(Worship)
PROVERBS 1:7; 9:10	(Wisdom)
ECCLESIATES 1:14; 3:14; 12:13-14	(Vanity)
SONG OF SOLOMON 2:16; 6:3; 8:6	(Beloved)
ISAIAH 6:3; 53:6	(Salvation)
JEREMIAH 1:10; 3:12,22	(Warning)
LAMENTATIONS 1:5; 2:17; 3:22	(Destruction)
EZEKIEL 1:1, 28b	(Visions)
DANIEL 4:17; 9:24-27	(Prophecy)
HOSEA 3:1; 6:4; 10;12	(Return)
JOEL 2:21, 32a	(Judgment)
AMOS 1:2; 4:12; 5:4	(Punishment)
OBADIAH 1:15	(Edom)
JONAH 2:9; 4:2b, 11a	(Repent)
MICAH 6:8; 7:18	(Controversy)
NAHUM 1:3, 7-8	(Nineveh)
HABAKKUK 2:2, 4, 20; 3:2	(Faith)
ZEPHANIAH 1:15: 2:3	(Remnant)
HAGGAI 1:8	(Build)
ZECHARIAH 8:3; 14:9	(Jealous)
MALACHI 3:1,8	(Robbery)
MATTHEW 1:1; 2:2; 28:18-20	(King)
MARK 10:45; 16:15	(Servant)
LUKE 19:10; 24:46-48	(Man)
JOHN 1:1-3,14; 20:30-31	(Savior)

ACTS 1:8; 2:41-47	(Witness)
ROMANS 1:16-17	(Righteousness)
I CORINTHIANS 1:10; 15:57-58	(Carnality)
II CORINTHIANS 4:5; 5:20-21; 9:15	(Defense)
GALATIANS 1:6-7; 5:1	(Liberty)
EPHESIANS 1:22-23; 2:19-20	(Church)
PHILIPPIANS 1:21; 4:13	(Rejoice)
COLOSSIANS 2:6-7; 3:1-2	(Knowledge)
I THESSALONIANS 4:16-17; 5:23	(Waiting)
II THESSALONIANS 2:1-3	(Revelation)
I TIMOTHY 4:16	(Godliness)
II TIMOTHY 4:5	(Doctrine)
TITUS 2:10; 3:14	(Good Works)
PHILEMON 1:10,18	(Intercession)
HEBREWS 1:1-2; 4:14; 11:1	(Better)
JAMES 1:2; 2:26	(Works)
I PETER 1:7; 5:7	(Suffering)
II PETER 2: 1-2	(Diligence)
I JOHN 1:7,9; 4:7,10	(Know)
II JOHN 1:2	(Walk)
III JOHN 1:2,4	(Truth)
JUDE 3, 20-21, 24-25	(Contend)
REVELATION 1: 1,19; 19:11; 21:1	(Reveal)

Appendix II

The Message of the Bible

JOHN 3:16 "For God so loved the world that He gave His only begotten Son, that whoever believes in Him should not perish but have everlasting life."

JOHN 20:30-31 "And truly Jesus did many other signs in the presence of His disciples, which are not written in this book; but these are written that you may believe that Jesus is the Christ, the Son of God, and that believing you may have life in His name."

HOW YOU CAN BELIEVE IN JESUS:

Admit that you are a sinner before God...
"For all have sinned and come short of the glory of God" (Romans 3:23)

Believe that Jesus died for you and arose from the dead to provide you victory over sin...
"But God while we were yet sinners, Christ died for us" (Romans 5:8)

Confess Christ as your personal Savior ...
"That if you confess with your mouth the Lord Jesus and believe in your heart....you will be saved." (Romans 10:9-10)

A SUGGESTED PRAYER TO RECEIVE JESUS:

"Dear Heavenly Father, I know You love me. I know I'm a sinner. I believe that Jesus died for my sins. I believe Jesus rose from the dead. I now receive Your Son, Jesus, as my personal Savior. Thank you for making me Your child. Help me to grow in my faith. In Jesus' name, Amen!"

FOR ASSURANCE OF SALVATION AND SPIRITUAL GROWTH:
READ I John 5:13 and Colossians 2:6-7

Diagram I
The Library of the Bible Books

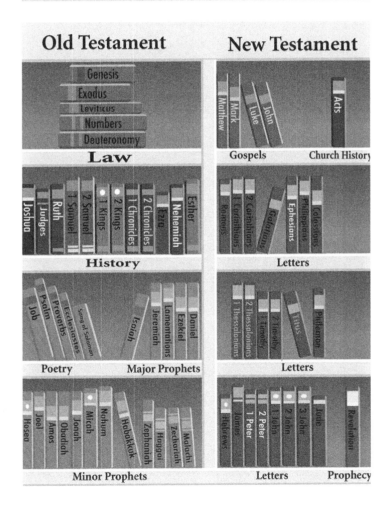